First Published in the UK in 2015 by Focus Education (UK) Ltd

Focus Education (UK) Ltd
Publishing
Talking Point Conference & Exhibition Centre
Huddersfield Road
Scouthead
Saddleworth
OL4 4AG

Focus Education (UK) Ltd Reg. No 4507968

ISBN 978-1-909038-74-5

Companies, institutions and other organisations wishing to make bulk purchases of books published by Focus Education should contact their local bookstore or Focus Education direct: Customer Services, Focus Education, Talking Point Conference & Exhibition Centre, Huddersfield Road, Scouthead, Saddleworth, OL4 4AG
Tel 01457 821818 Fax 01457 878205

www.focus-education.co.uk
customerservice@focus-education.co.uk
Printed in Great Britain by Focus Education UK Ltd, Scouthead

focuseducationuk

focuseducation1

focus-education-uk-ltd

ABOUT THE AUTHOR

Clive Davies, OBE is one of the founding Directors of Focus working with school both nationally and internationally. He draws on a vast experience, including work as a headteacher, Ofsted inspector, trainer and consultant.

Clive has a wealth of experience working with schools to analyse their current position and supporting leaders to construct purposeful and fit-for-purpose self-evaluation systems which impact on pupil outcomes. Over recent years, Clive has been focusing particularly on the development of an approach to leading and delivering the curriculum which ensures a high degree of engagement for children. This approach to the curriculum is being used in schools across England. He is one of the innovators for the learning challenge curriculum which has gained national acclaim for its success. Clive works in all areas of school improvement and works from early years through the secondary phase.

As a headteacher, Clive's school gained a National Curriculum Award and featured in the TES as one of three schools recognised for its quality practice. Clive has a national and international reputation as an authoritative speaker. He has recently worked in the Middle East, Europe and Japan.

Clive has written a wide range of publications which have become known for their straight forward and useful style; helping school leaders focus on what is most important to making a difference, including the best-selling 'Raising Standards by Setting Targets'. Some of Clive's most recent and bestselling publications are:

- Making Good Lessons Outstanding
- Maths Learning Challenge Curriculum: Pre and Post Learning Challenges
- Talk for Success
- Science Learning Challenge Curriculum
- History & Geography Learning Challenge Curriculum
- Leading the EYFS (co-authored with Sarah Quinn)
- Assessing Science and Non-Core Subjects: in the new National Curriculum (Years 1 to 6)
- Focus on Maths (co-authored with Helen Rowland)
- Assessing without Levels
- Empowering Learners: A Focus on Learning Behaviours
- Step up to the Challenge Series
- Making Book Scrutiny more Meaningful

Introduction: Mastery in Mathematics

This booklet aims to provide teachers in Year 3 & 4 with ideas to help develop pupils' mastery skills in mathematics. They are intended to be used alongside units of mathematics that are on-going in the classroom. For example, when pupils are being taught 'Place Value' teachers could choose an appropriate question to help deepen pupils' understanding of that aspect of mathematics.

Importantly, these should be used with all pupils not just the most able.
They should also be interwoven into everyday mathematics lessons not just left until the end of each unit.

The examples have been split into different areas so as to help teachers with their planning. Naturally, some examples cover more than one area.
The questions are simply exemplars and teachers are encouraged to develop questions that are similar to the ones outlined in this booklet. The questions take full account of the need for pupils to 'think harder' and to use their reasoning skills.

Possible Characteristics of Mastery	
Independence	Can apply the skill or knowledge without referring to the teacher.
Fluency	Can apply the skill or knowledge with a high level of confidence.
Application	Can apply the skill or knowledge to a range of different contexts, including other areas of the curriculum.
Consistency	Can use of their skills and understanding consistently.
Synthesis	Can organise ideas, information, or experiences into new, more complex interpretations and relationships.
Re-visit	Can return to this aspect of learning after a break and still feel confident that they can work on the skill or knowledge without difficulty.

When considering deep learning opportunities teachers need to ensure that the activities are enhancing the characteristics outlined above.

MASTERY IN MATHEMATICS

Year 3

YEAR 3 EXPECTATIONS

Year 3 Expectations

	PV	• Compare and order numbers to 1000 and read and write numbers to 1000 in numerals and words
	PV	• Count from 0 in multiples of 4, 8, 50 and 100
	PV	• Recognise the value of each digit in a 3-digit number
	AS	• Add and subtract mentally combinations of 1-digit and 2-digit numbers
	AS	• Add and subtract numbers with up to 3-digits using formal written methods
	AS	• Solve number problems using one and two step operation
	MD	• Derive and recall multiplication facts for 3, 4 and 8x multiplication tables
	MD	• Write and calculate mathematical statements for multiplication and division; including 2-digit number with a 1-digit number (from multiplication tables they know, ie, 2, 3, 4, 5, 8 and 10)
	F	• Understand and count in tenths, and find the fractional value of a given set
	F	• Add and subtract fractions with a common denominator
	G	• Identify right angles; compare other angles to being greater or smaller than a right angle
	G	• Identify horizontal and vertical lines and pairs of perpendicular and parallel lines
	M	• Tell time to nearest minute and use specific vocabulary: seconds, am and pm
	M	• Measure, compare, add and subtract using common metric measures
	S	• Solve one-step and two step problems using information presented in scaled bar charts, pictograms and tables

Year 3: Place Value

Place Value
Count from 0 in multiples of 4, 8, 50 and 100. Find 10 or 100 more or less than a given number.
Recognise the place value of each digit in a three-digit number (hundreds, tens, ones).
Compare and order numbers up to 1000. Read and write numbers up to 1000 in numerals and in words.
Identify, represent and estimate numbers using different representations.
Solve number problems and practical problems involving these ideas.

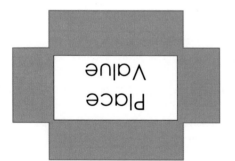

Place Value

Creating 3-digit numbers

Make up a 3-digit number where the sum of the numbers is 9, e.g. 333 or 450.

What is the largest number you can make?

What is the second largest number you can make?

True or false

Circle either True or False against each number statement

25 is one half of 50	True or False	
75 is a multiple of 5	True or False	
75 is the same as 24 times 3	True or False	
105 is half of 220	True or False	

Creating 3-digit numbers

Make up a 3-digit number where the sum of the numbers is 5, e.g. 122 or 212.

What is the largest number you can make?

What is the second largest number you can make?

Spot the mistake

What is wrong with these sequences of numbers?

50, 100, 115, 200

75, 100, 125, 150, 165, 200

In a science lesson children measure their height and weight. Here is a chart of their results.

Name	Weight (kg)	Height (cm)
Luke	52	98
Kaymer	58	102
Grace	47	89
George	71	110
Kane	65	105

Who is the heaviest person?
Who is the shortest person?
Luke grows 10cm. How tall is he now?

Chasing Shadows

At different times of the day pupils measured the length of their shadows. The table shows the outcomes:

Pupil Name	Length of shadow (cms)		
	8am	12 noon	6pm
Ahmed	205	145	215
Lucy	198	136	206
David	176	121	182
Tim	215	151	226

Say which person's shadow was the longest and when.

_____

Work out who the tallest person is.

_____

At what time of day are shadows longest?

_____

What is the difference between the shadow of the tallest person at 6pm and the shortest person at 12 noon?

_____

Creating 3-digit numbers

Look at the number cards below. Using the cards make up two 3-digit numbers that are more than 100 apart.	Look at the number cards below. Using the cards make up two 3-digit numbers that are less than 100 apart.
9 8 5 3 4	9 8 5 3 4

Look at the number cards below. Using the cards make up two 3-digit numbers that are more than 50 apart.	Look at the number cards below. Using the cards make up two 3-digit numbers that are less than 50 apart.
9 8 5 3 4	9 8 5 3 4

What's the answer?

6 children were given a maths problem where the answer was 198. Ariana put down 155 as her answer; George put down 183; Jemma put down 208; Hamid put down 217; Harry put down 164 and Mustafa put down 198. Who was closest to the answer and who was furthest away?	5 children were given a maths problem where the answer was 487. Harry put down 385 as his answer; James put down 473; Jen put down 618; Ahmed put down 592 and Harriet put down 464. Who was closest to the answer and who was furthest away?

More 3-digit numbers

Create 3-digit numbers where the unit is one less than the tens and the tens is one less than the hundreds. What are the largest and smallest possible numbers you can create?

Largest	Smallest

Create two 3-digit numbers that have a difference of more than 10 with the ones number being 7 and the hundreds number being 6?

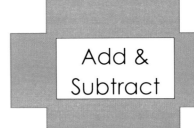

Add &
Subtract

Year 3: Add & Subtract

Add and Subtract	Add and subtract numbers mentally, including: a 3-digit no and 1s, 10s, 100s.
	Add and subtract numbers with up to 3 digits, using formal written methods of columnar addition and subtraction.
	Estimate the answer to a calculation and use inverse operations to check answers.
	Solve problems, including missing no problems, using number facts, place value, and more complex addition/subtraction.

Making an estimate

Which of these number sentences have the answer that is between 50 and 60

174 - 119
333 - 276
932 - 871

Always, sometimes, never

Is it always, sometimes or never true that if you subtract a multiple of 10 from any number the units digit of that number stays the same? Circle your answer.

always   sometimes   never

True or false

Are these number sentences true or false? Give your reasons.

597 + 7 = 614
804 - 70 = 744
768 + 140 = 908

Hard or easy?

Explain why you think the hard questions are hard?

323 + 10 =
393 + 10 =
454 - 100 =
954 - 120 =

Missing digits

___ + ___ + ___ = 201

Each missing digit is either a 9 or a 1. Write in the missing digits. Can you find different ways of doing this?

Making an estimate

Which of these number sentences have the answer that is between 50 and 60
194 - 149
433 – 376
732 – 571

Always, sometimes, never

Is it always, sometimes or never true that if you subtract a multiple of 10 from any number the units digit of that number stays the same?

always   sometimes   never

Is it always, sometimes or never true that when you add two numbers together you will get an even number?

always   sometimes   never

Toy shop

Here are the prices of items in a toy shop. You have £15 to spend. Write below which toys you can afford to buy whilst leaving yourself no more than £2 in change.

Model car	doll	Train set	puzzle	jigsaw
£2	£4	£5	£2	£1

Magic set	Ball	Skipping rope	Cricket set	Goalposts
£6	£2	£2	£10	£11

Which toys have you bought? (Don't forget they can't total more than £15.)

You have 3 friends to buy for and your parents say you cannot spend more than £20. Make a list of your purchases.

Friend A _____

Friend B _____

Friend C _____

The dice game

I have 8 dice (1 to 6). Show three ways I can lay out the dice so that numbers on top add up to 32.

I have 10 dice (1 to 6). Show three ways I can lay out the dice so that numbers on top add up to 43.

The two opposite sides of a dice always add up to 7. If the top numbers of 3 dice are 4, 2 and 5, how much will the bottom numbers add up to?

Cafe

At the café, next to school, you can buy the following:

Drink	Snack	Lunch
Tea 40p	Crisps 35p	Burger 75p
Coke 25p	Biscuits 20p	Sausage Roll 45p
Coffee 40p	Sweets 25p	Chips 35p
Milk 20p	Apple 15p	Bacon Roll 55p
Water 10p		
Orange Juice 15p		

You have £1 to spend. Choose 1 item from each group to buy. List them below and then work out how much they cost you altogether. How much change you will have from £1?

Drink	Snack	Lunch

Total Cost

Change

Relay run

Four runners each ran 100m in a relay. The first runner took 16 seconds; the second 15 seconds; the third 18 seconds and the last runner took 14 seconds. How long did it take for the runners to complete the relay?

The four runners completed the relay in 78 seconds. The fastest runner ran her leg twice as fast as the slowest runner and the other two ran their leg in the same time. How fast did each runner run? Give one possible solution.

The 25 Dice trick

25 dice are placed together as below. All dice have numbers 1 to 6.

Set out the dice in any way you want in another 5 x 5 pattern so that the numbers facing upwards add up to 125.

Set out the dice in any way you want in another 5 x 5 pattern so that the numbers facing upwards add up to 105.

Set out the dice in any way you want in a 6 x 6 pattern so that the numbers facing upwards add up to 125.

Set out the dice in any way you want in a 4 x 4 pattern so that the numbers facing upwards add up to 56.

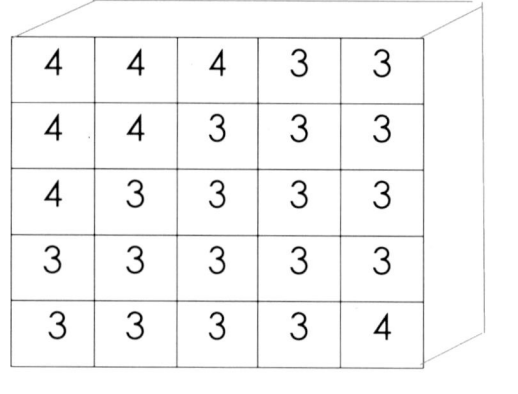

4	4	4	3	3
4	4	3	3	3
4	3	3	3	3
3	3	3	3	3
3	3	3	3	4

Triangle fun

Look at the example on the left hand side below. Complete the problem on the right hand side, putting the correct numbers in the empty squares.

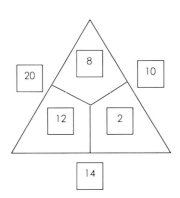

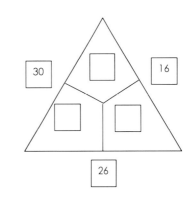

More triangle fun

Look at the example on the left hand side below. Complete the problem on the right hand side, putting the correct numbers in the empty squares.

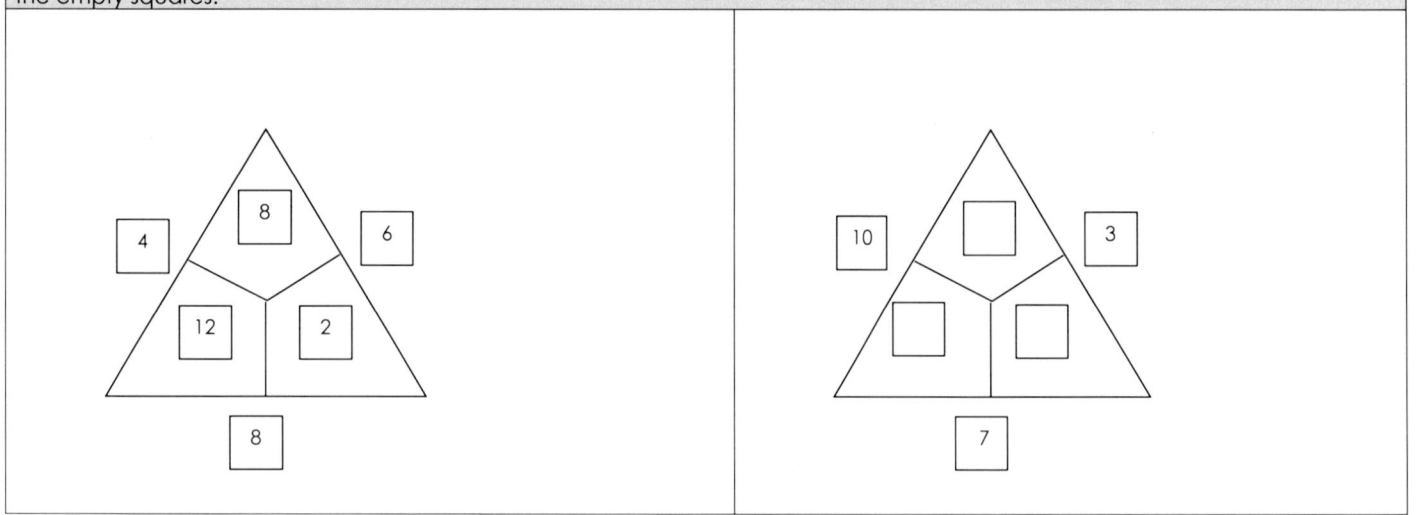

Dart board problem

A special dart board has 8 numbers from 10 to 45 going up in 5s.

If the dart hits a segment in the blue area the number doubles so the highest possible number could be 90.

How many ways could the 3 darts be placed to score exactly 200? Write out all possibly combinations.

How many ways can you score 150?

Set out your combinations.

How many ways could you score 100?

Set out your combinations

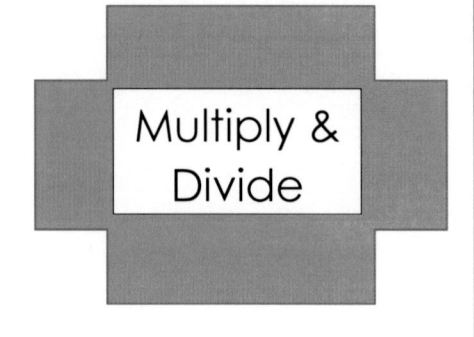

Multiply &
Divide

Year 3: Multiply & Divide

Multiply & Divide	Recall and use multiplication and division facts for the 3, 4 and 8 multiplication tables.
	Write and calculate math statements for x and ÷ using the tables they know, including 2-digit numbers times 1-digit numbers, using mental and formal written methods.
	Solve problems and missing number problems, involving x and ÷, including integer scaling problems and correspondence problems in which n objects are connected to m objects.

How close can you get?

☐ X ☐ = ☐

Using the digits 2, 3 and 4 in the calculation above. How close can you get to 100?

What is the largest product?

What is the smallest product?

☐ X ☐ = ☐

Using the digits 5, 6 and 7 in the calculation above. How close can you get to 200?

What is the largest product?

What is the smallest product?

Use the inverse

Use the inverse to check if the following calculations are correct.

23 x 4 = 82
117 ÷ 9 = 14

Size of an answer

Will the answer to the following calculations be greater or less than 80?

23 x 3=
32 x 3 =
42 x 3 =
36 x 2=

Checking cost

A class of 30 has planned a visit to a museum. If everyone pays the same to enter, how much money could be collected?

Put a tick or a cross against the possible answers.

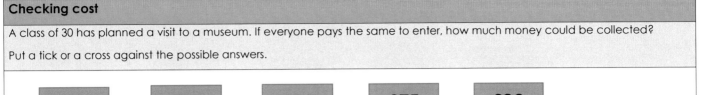

£30   £25   £60   £75   £29

A family of 4 decided to go to see the latest film about a Stone Age boy. Tickets for the adults cost twice as much as the tickets for the children. How much might the family have spent altogether?

£15   £34   £60   £23   £29

In a Mediterranean hotel a breakfast costs £5. The bill for the room and breakfasts, at the end of 7 days, costs £315. How much does the room cost each day?

Holiday

A family of 2 adults and 4 children go on holiday. The air tickets cost £105 for each adult and £72 for each child. The hotel bill is £250 for all of them. How much does the family spend altogether?

Dinosaur park

A group of adults and children decided to visit the dinosaur park. The adults paid twice as much as the children. The group paid £150. How many adults and children could have been in the group? Give two different answers.

Multiple triangles

Look at the example on the left hand side below. Complete the problem on the right hand side, putting the correct numbers in the empty squares.

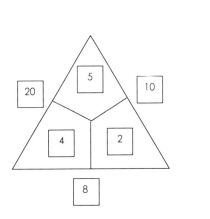

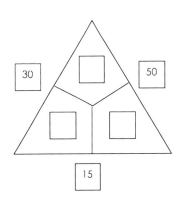

Dice multiplication and division

I threw 2 dice. The numbers when multiplied made 24. What were the numbers?	I threw 2 dice. The numbers when multiplied made 12. How many pairs of numbers could there have been? What are they?
I threw 2 dice. The numbers when divided made 2. What were the possible combination of the dice numbers?	I threw 2 dice. The numbers when divided made 3. What were the possible combination of the dice numbers?

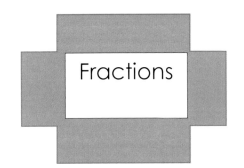

Fractions

Year 3: Fractions

Fractions	Count up and down in tenths; recognise that tenths arise from dividing an object into 10 equal parts and in dividing one-digit numbers or quantities by 10.
	Recognise, find and write fractions of a discrete set of objects: unit fractions and non-unit fractions with small denominators.
	Recognise and use fractions as numbers: unit fractions and non-unit fractions with small denominators.
	Recognise and show, using diagrams, equivalent fractions with small denominators.
	Add and sub fractions with the same denominator within one whole (e.g. $\frac{5}{7} + \frac{1}{7} = \frac{6}{7}$).
	Compare and order unit fractions, and fractions with the same denominators.

Ordering

Put these fractions in the correct order, starting with the smallest.

4/8   3/4   1/4

What do you notice?

Continue the pattern

1/10 + 9/10 = 1
2/10 + 8/10 = 1
3/10 + 7/10 = 1

Make up a similar pattern for eighths.

Gardening

A gardener has been very busy planting seeds. Work out how many of these become full grown plants by looking at the table below.

No of seeds	1500	500	300	1000
Name of plant	peas	pansies	cress	sunflowers
Fraction germinated	1/2	1/5	2/3	3/4
Answer				

Bowl of Fruit

One eighth of a bowl of fruit was made up of bananas. A quarter was made up of pears and a half was made up of apples.	One tenth of a bowl of fruit was made up of kiwi fruit. Three tenths was made up of pears and a half was made up of apples.
If there were no more than 30 pieces of fruit altogether, how many bananas, pears and apples could there have been in the fruit bowl?	If there were no more than 50 pieces of fruit altogether, how many kiwi fruit, pears and apples could there have been in the fruit bowl?

Garden centre

In a garden centre, the owner was working out how well his plants were selling. Work out how many of each plant he had sold.

Name of plant	Rose	Conifer bush	Camellia	Honeysuckle
Number of plants	60	60	30	40
Fraction sold	2/3	1/4	1/2	3/5
Answer				

In a forest

In a forest, the warden had to cut down a number of trees so that new ones could be planted. Work out how many of each type of tree is cut down.

No of trees	200	500	300	1000
Name of tree	pine	oak	birch	sycamore
Fraction to be cut down	1/2	2/5	2/3	1/4
Answer				

On a Farm

On a farm there were sheep; chickens; cows and horses. 1/2 of the animals were sheep, 1/3 were chickens, 1/10 were cows and the rest were horses.

If the farm had more than 200 animals but less than 230, how many sheep, chickens, cows and horses were there on the farm?

If there were more than 250 animals altogether but less than 280, how many sheep, chickens, cows and horses were there?

Year 3: Measures

Measures	Know the number of seconds in a minute and the number of days in each month, year and leap year.
	Estimate and read time with increasing accuracy, to nearest min; record/compare time in seconds, minutes, hrs. Use vocabulary such as o'clock, am/pm, morning, afternoon, noon and midnight.
	Tell/write the time from an analogue clock, including Roman numerals from I to XII, and 12-hr/24-hr clocks.
	Add and subtract amounts of money to give change, using both £ and p in practical contexts.
	Measure the perimeter of simple 2-D shapes.
	Measure, compare, add and subtract: lengths (m/cm/mm); mass (kg/g); volume/capacity (l/ml).

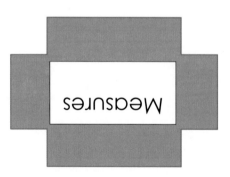

Measures

Ordering

Put these measurements in order starting with the largest.

Half a litre	500 metres
Quarter of a litre	1Km
300 ml	5000 cms

Position the symbols

Place the correct symbol between the measurements > or <

306 cm ▢ Half a metre
930 ml ▢ 1 litre

Explain your thinking

Undoing

A television programme lasting 45 minutes finished at 5.20. At what time did it start?

Draw a clock to show the start and finish times.

Perimeter

The side of a square is equivalent to a whole number (in cms). Which of the following measurements could represent its perimeter?

8cm   18cm   24cm   25cm

Write more statements

(You may choose to consider this practically)

If there are 630ml of water in a jug, how much water do you need to add to make a litre of water?

What if there was 450 ml to start with? Make up some more questions like this

Explain thinking

Salha says that 100 minutes is the same as 1 hour.

Is Salha right? Explain your answer.

Possibilities

I bought a book which cost between £9 and £10 and I paid with a ten pound note.
My change was between 50p and £1 and was all in silver coins. What price could I have paid?

The answer is...

25 minutes	45 minutes
What is the question?	What is the question?

What do you notice?

1 minute = 60 seconds   2 minutes = 120 seconds

Continue the pattern.   Write down some more time facts like these.

Time and time again

How many hours are there in 2 days?	How many hours are there in 1 week?

It is now half past eight.

Helen has to be home by 11 o'clock and she is watching a film at her friend's house which lasts 2 hours. It takes 10 minutes to walk home.

Has she enough time to watch all the film?

It is now one o'clock.

Paul has to be home by half past three.

He is playing football for his team. The game lasts for 1 and a half hours. It takes half an hour to have a shower after the game and 15 minutes to get home.

Has he enough time to get home on time?

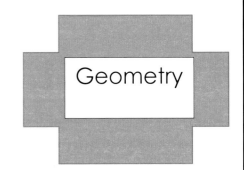

Geometry

Year 3: Geometry

Geometry	Draw 2-D shapes and make 3-D shapes using modelling materials; recognise 3-D shapes in different orientations and describe them.
	Recognise that angles are a property of shape or a description of a turn.
	Identify right angles, recognise that 2 right angles make a half-turn, 3 make three quarters of a turn and 4 a complete turn. Identify whether angles are greater than or less than a right angle.
	Identify horizontal and vertical lines and pairs of perpendicular and parallel lines.

Visualising 3-D shapes

I am thinking of a 3-dimensional shape which has faces that are triangles and squares.
What could my shape be?

One face of a 3-D shape looks like this.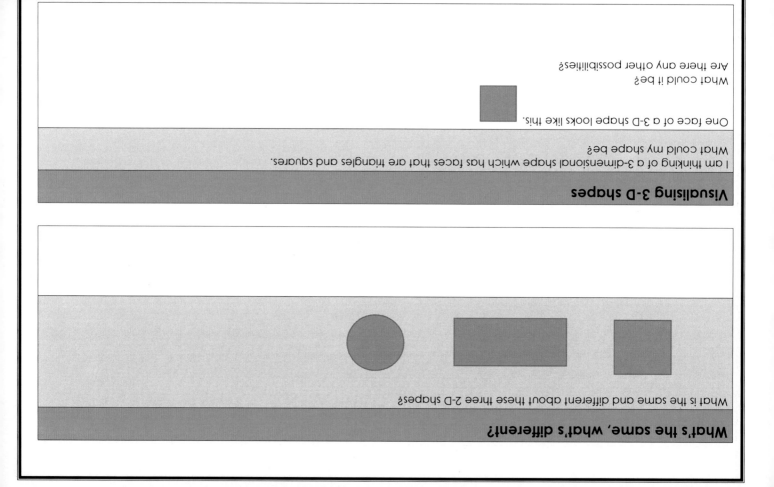
What could it be?
Are there any other possibilities?

What's the same, what's different?

What is the same and different about these three 2-D shapes?

Always, sometimes, never

Is it always, sometimes or never that all sides of a hexagon are the same length.

always   sometimes   never

Perpendicular or parallel

Which capital letters have perpendicular and / or parallel lines?

Working backwards

If I make the two opposite sides of a square 5 cm longer the new lengths of those sides are 27cm.
What was the length of the side of my original square?
What is the name and length of sides of my new shape?

Drawing horizontal or vertical lines

Below, draw a horizontal line that is 5cm long and a vertical line that is 3 cm long.

Overlapping squares

How many squares can you make by overlapping 3 squares of the same size?

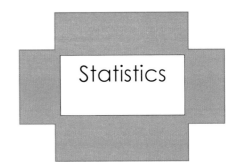

Statistics

Year 3: Statistics

| Stats | Interpret and present data using bar charts, pictograms and tables. |
| | Solve one-step and two-step questions such as 'How many more?' and 'How many fewer?' using information presented in scaled bar charts, pictograms and tables. |

Science Lessons

In a science lesson children are looking at muscles and skeletons. They try to find out how much weight they can lift from the floor to their tummies. Here is a chart of their results.

Name	Weight (kg)
Pedro	18
Amir	23
Charlotte	17
India	19
Teacher	34

Who can lift the heaviest weight?

How much can India and Charlotte lift altogether?

Calculate the difference between the person who can lift the most and the person who can lift the least.

Television kids

Children in a class talk about how much television they watch each week. They decide to keep a record for 3 weeks and then put their information on this chart.

Pupil Name	Number of hours watched each week		
	Week 1	Week 2	Week 3
Danny	18	19	21
Libby	1	13	20
Hannah	17	12	18
Tony	30	15	36

Who watched most television over 3 weeks?

Which week was the most popular for watching television?

How many hours television did Hannah watch altogether?

Why might Libby have watched only 1 hour of television in Week 1?

Mini olympics

In a mini Olympics event at school children score 3 points for coming first; 2 points for coming second and 1 point for coming third. Have a look at the chart below and then answer the questions.

Name	Running	Jumping	Throwing	Catching
Raisa		3rd		3rd
Helen	1st			
Tom			1st	
Amid	2nd	1st	2nd	1st
Ryan	3rd			
Ellie		2nd	3rd	2nd

Who won the running event?

Who won most events?

How many points did Ellie have altogether?

How many points did the winner collect?

Homework

Children in a class talk about the amount of time they spend doing homework. They decide to keep a record for 3 weeks and then put their information on this chart.

Pupil Name	Number of hours doing homework each week		
	Week 1	Week 2	Week 3
Sian	8	3	8
Ramesa	1	1	1
Richard	7	4	7
Billie	3	2	3

Create a block graph to show the number of hours spent by the four children doing homework during week 1.

Create another block graph to show how much homework Richard did over the 3 weeks.

(You should use squared paper to complete these graphs.)

Give a good reason why Ramesa only did 1 hour homework during weeks 1, 2 and 3.

MASTERY IN MATHEMATICS

Year 4

YEAR 4 EXPECTATIONS

Year 4 Expectations

	PV	• Round any number to the nearest 10, 100 or 1000 and decimals with one decimal place to the nearest whole number
	PV	• Count backwards through zero to include negative numbers
	AS	• Solve addition and subtraction two-step problems in context and solve problems involving multiplication and division
	MD	• Multiply 2-digit and 3-digit numbers by a 1-digit number using formal written layout
	MD	• Recall all multiplication facts to 12 x 12
	F	• Solve simple measures and money problems involving fractions and decimals to 2 decimal places
	F	• Compare numbers with the same number of decimal places up to 2 decimal places
	F	• Recognise and write decimal equivalents of any number of tenths or hundredths
	F	• Add and subtract with up to 4 decimal places using formal written methods of columnar addition and subtraction
	F	• Divide a 1 or 2-digit number by 10 or 100 identifying the value of the digits in the answer as units, tenths and hundredths
	G	• Compare and classify geometrical shapes, including quadrilaterals and triangles, based on their properties and sizes
	G	• Know that angles are measured in degrees and identify acute and obtuse angles and compare and order angles up to two right angles by size
	M	• Measure and calculate the perimeter of a rectilinear figure in centimetres and metres
	M	• Read, write and convert between analogue and digital 12 and 24 hour clocks

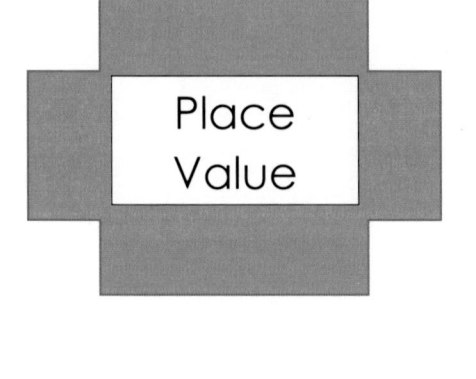

Place
Value

Year 4: Place Value

Place Value	Count in multiples of 6, 7, 9, 25 and 1000.
	Find 1000 more or less than a given number. Round any number to the nearest 10, 100 or 1000.
	Count backwards through zero to include negative numbers.
	Recognise the place value of each digit in a 4-digit number (thousands, hundreds, tens, and ones). Order and compare numbers beyond 1000.
	Read Roman numerals to 100 (I to C) and know that over time, the numeral system changed to include the concept of zero and place value.

Spot the mistake

950, 975, 1000, 1250

What is wrong with this sequence of numbers?

True or false

324 is a multiple of 9?

What comes next?

6706+ 1000= 7706
7706 + 1000 = 8706
8706 + 1000 = 9706

Explain the order

5035, 5053, 5350, 5530, 5503
If you wrote these numbers in order, starting with the largest, which number would be third?
Explain how you ordered the numbers.

Digital value

Show the value of the digit 4 in these numbers.
3041 4321 5497
Explain how you know.

Create your own numbers

Create four-digit numbers where the digit sum is six and the tens digit is one.
eg 2211, 4110, 3210
What is the largest/smallest number you can make?

Rounding

A number, rounded to the nearest ten, is 540. What is the smallest possible number it could be?	Round 296 to the nearest 10. Round it to the nearest 100. What do you notice? Suggest other numbers like this.

Rounding

A number, rounded to the nearest ten, is 780. What is the smallest possible number it could be?	Round 797 to the nearest 10. Round it to the nearest 100. What do you notice? Suggest other numbers like this.

Creating 4-digit numbers

Make up a 4-digit number where the sum of the numbers is 9, e.g. 3312 or 4500.

What is the largest number you can make?	What is the second largest number you can make?
What is the smallest number you can make?	**What is the second smallest number you can make?**

Making up 2-digit numbers

Look at the number cards below. Using the cards make up 2 ThHTU (4-digit numbers) that are more than 1000 apart.	Look at the number cards below. Using the cards make up 2 ThHTU (4-digit numbers) that are less than 1000 apart.
9 8 5 3 4	9 8 5 3 4

Who is nearest?

6 children were given a maths problem where the answer was -7. Ariana wrote -15 as her answer; George wrote +3; Jemma wrote -2; Hamid wrote +1; Harry wrote -6 and Mustafa wrote zero. Who was closest to the answer and who was furthest away?	5 children were given a maths problem where the answer was 4870. Harry wrote 3858 as his answer; wrote 4735; Jen wrote 6187; Ahmed wrote 5925 and Harriet wrote 4648. Who was closest to the answer and who was furthest away?

Creating 4-digit numbers

Create 4-digit numbers where the unit is one less than the tens and the hundreds is one less than the thousands. What is the largest possible number, and what is the smallest number, you can create?

Largest	Smallest

Create two 4-digit numbers that have a difference of more than 10 and the ones number is 9 and the hundreds number is 8?

Year 4: Addition and Subtraction

Add and Subtract	Add and subtract numbers with up to 4 digits using the formal written methods of columnar addition and subtraction where appropriate.	
	Estimate and use inverse operations to check answers to a calculation.	
	Solve addition and subtraction two-step problems in contexts, deciding which operations and methods to use and why.	

Addition & Subtraction

Buying options

Andrew has to buy 3 presents for his sisters, Mary, Helen and Faye. He has a total of £50 to spend. Choose 3 presents from the list below and show how much change there will be?

Mary	Cost
Coat	£23
Jumper	£16.50
Hair Accessories	£14
Dress	£20.50
Helen	
Talking Doll	£16.50
Toy Pushchair	£19.50
Doll's House	£23.50
Toy Computer	£13.50
Faye	
Large Teddy Bear	£13.50
Mini Farm	£17
Selection of Games	£15.50
Toy tape recorder	£21

Select a gift for each sister. Write the gifts below making sure that the total does not come to more than £50.

How much change will there be?

Science experiment

During a science experiment a group of children wanted to find out how far sound travels. On an **open field** they could hear each other over a distance of 83 metres; in a **crowded street** they could hear each other over a distance of 18 metres; inside a **busy school** they could hear each other over a distance of 6 metres; and in the **middle of a wood** they could hear each other over a distance of 25 metres.

Work out the difference between the distances that they could hear each other in an **open field** and the **middle of a wood**.

In which two locations could the children hear each other if they were 20 metres apart?

Dice game

I have 10 dice (1 to 6). Show three ways I can lay out the dice so that the numbers on top add up to 36.

I have 12 dice (1 to 6). Show three ways I can lay out the dice so that the numbers on top add up to 60.

The two opposite sides of a dice always add up to 7. If the top numbers of 5 dice are 4, 2, 1 5 and 5, how much will the bottom numbers add up to?

African safari

A family went on a special African safari holiday. At the resort the family were offered a number of excursions. The costs are set out below:

Excursion	Safari overnight camp	Elephant Lake	Lion Park
Adult	£250	£120	£60
Child	£175	£80	£40
Family ticket	£650	£280	£105

How much will it cost for a family ticket for the overnight safari and for 2 adults to go to the lion park?

Is it cheaper for a family of 2 adults and 2 children:
   a)   to go on the overnight safari,
   b)   or for 2 adults to go to the elephant lake and for 2 children to go to the lion park

Summer camp

Children have to buy outfits for their summer camp. Each child needs a sweat shirt; shorts and shoes. The choices are set out below.

Sweatshirt	Cost
Extra warm	£30
Cotton	£15
Wool	£24
Short sleeves	£22
Shorts	
Designer	£16
White	£11
Blue	£13
With a badge	£19
Shoes	
Trainers	£23
Black	£15
Sandals	£13
Jelly	£10

How much will the cheapest option cost altogether? Use the area below to show your workings.

How much will the most expensive option cost altogether? Use the space below to show your workings.

You have a budget of £50. Calculate what you can afford and show how much change you will have from £50.

True or false

Are these number sentences true or false?

$6.7 + 0.4 = 6.11$
$8.1 - 0.9 = 7.2$

Give your reasons.

Hard or easy

Which questions are easiest/hardest?

$1323 - 70 =$
$12893 + 300 =$
$19354 - 500 =$
$19954 + 100 =$

Explain why you think the hard questions are hard.

Convince me

$\square - 666 = \square\,8\,\square\,5$

What is the largest possible number that will go in the rectangular box?

What is the smallest?

Convince me

Making an estimate

Which of these number sentences have the answer that is between 550 and 600?

1174 – 611

3330 – 2779

9326 – 8777

Always, sometimes, never

Is it always, sometimes or never true that the difference between two odd numbers is odd?

4	1	4	3	3
4	5	3	3	2
4	5	3	3	3
3	5	3	6	3
3	2	3	3	4

25 dice are placed together as above. All dice have numbers 1 to 6. The number directly beneath the number seen, when added to the number seen, always adds up to 7. In other words each of the 3s seen above will have a 4 directly underneath, each of the 5s seen will have a 2 directly beneath and the 6 will have a 1 beneath, etc.

Set out the dice pattern as above but this time show the numbers underneath. For example, your first row should be 3, 6, 3, 4 and 4.

Set out the dice in any way you want in another 5 x 5 pattern so that the numbers underneath add up to 105.

Set out the dice in any way you want in a 6 x 6 pattern so that the numbers underneath add up to 125.

Set out the dice in any way you want in a 4 x 4 pattern so that the numbers underneath add up to 56.

Complicated triangles

Look at the example on the left hand side below. Complete the problem on the right hand side, putting the correct numbers in the empty squares.

More complicated triangles

Look at the example on the left hand side. Complete the problem on the right hand side, putting the correct numbers in the empty squares.

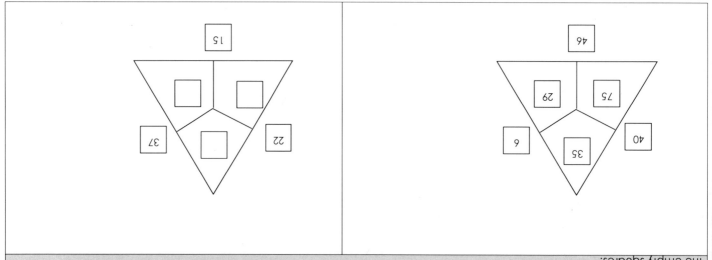

Creating numbers

Put any 4 numbers (0-9) into the empty spaces below. Then create 4 2-digit numbers as shown below.

Example   62 + 38 + 64 + 28 = 192

6	2
3	8

Put 4 numbers in the spaces below so that you get as close to 100 (in the first) and 200 (in the second) as you can.

Year 4: Multiplication & Division

Multiply and Divide	Recall multiplication and division facts for multiplication tables up to 12 × 12.
	Recognise and use factor pairs and commutativity in mental calculations.
	Multiply two-digit and three-digit numbers by a one-digit number using formal written layout.
	Solve problems involving x and +, including using the distributive law to multiply 2 digit numbers by 1 digit, integer scaling problems and harder correspondence problems such as n objects are connected to m objects.

Electric bills

The electricity bill for the school was £5,350 per year before they had solar panels. The school made a decision to buy 10 solar panels and this cut their bill to £2,100 per year. The solar panels cost £850 each.

How much did the solar panels cost altogether?

How much was the school's electricity bill for the 10 years before they had the solar panels?

How much did they spend for the 10 years after they bought the solar panels? Don't forget to add in the cost of buying the solar panels. (Show your working out.)

More electric bills

In a football stadium the electricity bill was £15,350 per year before they decided to buy special 'energy saving' lamps for their floodlights.

- The 'energy saving' bulbs cost £1,150 each and they had to buy 16 in total.
- After they had installed the new bulbs the electricity bill was reduced to £4,500 a year.

Work out the following:

How much did the 'energy saving' bulbs cost altogether?

How much was the football stadium's electricity bill for the 5 years before they had the new energy saving bulbs?

If you consider the 5 years before the energy saving bulbs were installed and the 5 years after the energy saving bulbs were installed, how much money will the football stadium have saved? Don't forget to add in the cost of buying the energy saving bulb. (Show your working out.)

Yet more electric bills

In a Garden Centre the electricity bill was £5,350 per year before they decided to buy special 'energy saving' lamps for their greenhouses.

- The 'energy saving' bulbs cost £150 each and they had to buy 30 in total.
- After they had installed the new bulbs the electricity bill was reduced to £1,550 a year.

Work out the following?

How much did the 'energy saving' bulbs cost altogether?

How much was the Garden Centre's electricity bill for the 5 years before they had the new energy saving bulbs?

If you consider the 5 years before the energy saving bulbs were installed, and the 5 years after the energy saving bulbs were installed, how much money will the Garden Centre have saved? Don't forget to add in the cost of buying the energy saving bulb. (Show your working out.)

Holiday time

A family are working out which is their best option for their Mediterranean holiday. The costs are set out below:

Hotel	All Inclusive for each person per week	Adult rate per day	Child Rate per day
Room	£1250	£120	£60
Breakfast		£10	£5
Lunch		£10	£5
Dinner		£20	£10

How much will it cost for a family of 4 to go 'All Inclusive' for one week?

Which is cheaper for a family of 2 adults and 2 children?
   a)   To all go 'all Inclusive' for the week (7 days),
   b)   Or to pay a daily rate and have breakfast; lunch and dinner each day. (Show your workings.)

How close can you get?

$$\boxed{}\ \boxed{} \quad \mathrm{X} \quad \boxed{} \quad = \quad \boxed{}$$

Using only the digits 2, 3, 4 and 5 in the calculation above how close can you get to 200?

What is the largest product you can make?

What is the smallest product you can make?

Missing numbers

$72 = \boxed{} \ \mathrm{X} \ \boxed{}$

Which pairs of numbers could be written in the boxes?

Making links

Eggs are bought in boxes of 12. I need 140 eggs. How many boxes will I need to buy?

Use a number fact

$63 \div 9 = 7$

Use this fact to work out:

$126 \div 9 =$

$252 \div 7 =$

Making more links

How can you use factor pairs to solve this calculation?

13×12

$(13 \times 3 \times 4,\ 13 \times 3 \times 2 \times 2,\ 13 \times 2 \times 6)$

Prove it

What goes in the missing box?

6 ▢ x 4 = 512

Prove it.

How close can you get?

▢ ▢ ▢ X 7

Using the digits 3, 4 and 6 in the calculation above how close can you get to 4500?

What is the largest product?

What is the smallest product?

Always, sometimes, never

Is it always, sometimes or never true that an even number divisible by 3, is also divisible by 6.

Always, sometimes, never

Is it always, sometimes or never true that the sum of four even numbers is divisible by 4.

Greater or less than

Will the answer to the following calculations be greater or less (<, >) than 300?

152 × 2=

78 × 3 =

87 × 3 =

4 × 74 =

Using the inverse

Use the inverse to check if the following calculations are correct.

23 x 4 = 92

117 ÷ 9 = 14

Multiplication triangles

Look at the example on the left hand side below. Complete the problem on the right hand side, putting the correct numbers in the empty squares.

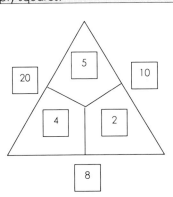

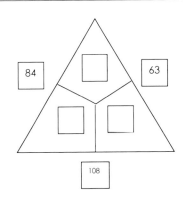

Positive and negative dice

You have 2 dice. 1 is numbered 1 to 6 and the second is numbered -1 to -6.

When throwing 2 dice the numbers when multiplied made -12. What were the two possible numbers you could have?

When throwing 2 dice the numbers when multiplied made -15. How many pairs of numbers could there have been? What are they?

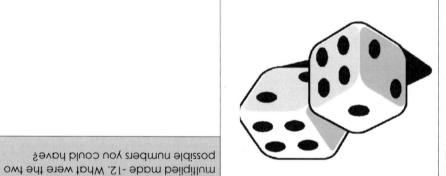

Multiple opportunities

A football team has the option of wearing 5 different tops, 4 different shorts and 3 sets of socks. One shirt is all white, one pair of shorts is white and one pair of socks is also white.

How many possible combinations of kit can they choose for any match?

If they had to wear the white shorts how many combinations can they now wear?

If they are not allowed to wear white shirts; white shorts or white socks, how many combinations are they able to choose from?

Year 4: Fraction

Fractions	Recognise and show, using diagrams, families of common equivalent fractions.
	Count up and down in hundredths; recognise that hundredths arise when dividing an object by a hundred and dividing tenths by ten.
	Add and subtract fractions with the same denominator.
	Recognise and write decimal equivalents of any number of tenths or hundredths; and the decimal equivalents to ¼, ½ and ¾.
	Find the effect of dividing a one- or two-digit number by 10 and 100, identifying the value of the digits in the answer as ones, tenths and hundredths.
	Round decimals with one decimal place to the nearest whole number. Solve simple measure and money problems involving fractions and decimals to 2 decimal places.

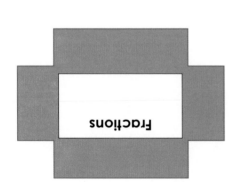

Fractions

The X Factor

After a special addition of the X Factor the favourite group 'Two Boys' had twice the number of downloads than 'Tricia' who had 836 downloads. 'No Direction' had half as many downloads as 'Two Boys' and 'Tricia' added together.

How many downloads did 'Two Boys' have?

How many downloads did No Direction have?

Spot the mistake

sixty tenths, seventy tenths, eighty tenths, ninety tenths, twenty tenths

… and correct it.

What comes next?

83/100, 82/100, 81/100, ….., ….., …..

31/100, 41/100, 51/100, ….., …..,

What do you notice?

1/10 of 100 = 10
1/100 of 100 = 1
2/10 of 100 = 20
2/100 of 100 = 2

How can you use this to work out: 6/10 of 200
6/100 of 200?

True or false

1/20 of a metre = 20cm

4/100 of 2 metres = 40cm

Find an example

Give an example of a fraction that is more than a half but less than a whole.

Now give another example that no one else will think of.

Explain how you know the fraction is more than a half but less than a whole. (Draw an image.)

Greater than or less than

Put the correct symbol < or > in each box

3.03 ▢ 3.33

0.37 ▢ 0.32

Adding or subtracting

What needs to be added to 3.23 to give 3.53?

What needs to be added to 3.16 to give 3.2?

Do, and then explain

Circle each decimal which when rounded to the nearest whole number is 5.

5.3   5.7   5.2   5.8

Explain your reasoning.

Complete the pattern

Complete the pattern by filling in the blank cells in this table:

0.1		0.3	
10/100	20/100		40/100
1/10	2/10	3/10	

What do you notice?

Find 4/6 of 24

Find 2/3 of 24

What do you notice?

Write any other similar statements.

Odd one out

Which is the odd one out in each of these trios?

3/4   9/12   4/6

9/12   10/15   2/3

Why?

Finding decimal places

Write a decimal number (to one decimal place) which lies between a half and three quarters.

Ordering

Put these numbers in the correct order, starting with the smallest.

    1/4   0.75   5/10

Explain your thinking

What do you notice?

5/5 – 1/5 = 4/5

4/5 – 1/5 = 3/5

What do you notice?

11/100 + 89/100 = 1

12/100 + 88/100 = 1

13/100 + 87/100 = 1

Continue the pattern for the next five number sentences

Undoing

I divide a number by 100 and the answer is 0.3. What number did I start with?

Approximate answer

Write down a number with one decimal place which, when multiplied by 10, gives an answer between 120 and 130.

Approximate answer

Write down a number with one decimal place which when multiplied by 10 gives an answer between 120 and 130.

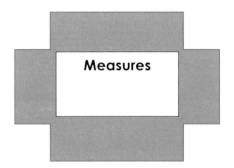

Measures

Year 4: Measures

Measures	Convert between different units of measure (e.g. kilometre to metre). Solve problems involving converting from hours to minutes; minutes to seconds; years to months; weeks to days).
	Measure and calculate the perimeter of a rectilinear figure (including squares) in centimetres and metres. Find the area of rectilinear shapes by counting squares.
	Estimate, compare and calculate different measures, including money in pounds and pence.
	Read, write and convert time between analogue and digital 12 and 24-hour clocks.

Healthy eating café

A new healthy eating café has just opened and this is its menu.

Starters	Cost
Goat cheese salad	£2.50
Melon and grapefruit cocktail	£2.25
Prawn cocktail	£2.45
Vegetable soup	£2.10
Main meal	
Tomato pasta bake	£5.50
Chicken salad	£6.75
Tuna salad	£6.90
Vegetable curry	£5.50
Dessert	
Yogurt	£1.50
Rice pudding	£1.75
Muesli	£2.00

Select a meal, which includes a starter, main meal and dessert costing you £15 or less?

How much change you will have from £15 (it may be 0p).

Holiday planning

When considering where to go on holiday in May, a family decided to check on the temperature, rainfall and the time it takes to get to different European cities so as to help them make up their mind where to go. The following chart gives details of their findings.

City	Time to get there (hours)	Rainfall (mm)	Temp (°c)
Paris	2	12	16
Munich	3	8	15
Antalya	5	1	28
Athens	5	1	25
Oslo	4	18	6

Mum wants a hot climate (at least more than 20) and isn't concerned about how long it takes to get there. What choices does she have?

Dad doesn't want to travel for more than 3 hours. What choices does he have?

Their son likes long flights but hates warm weather. Where could he choose to go?

Their daughter wants to go somewhere where she is not travelling more than 3 hours and where the rainfall is no more than 10mm. Where will she choose?

Ordering measures

Put these amounts in order starting with the largest.

Half of three litres
Quarter of two litres
300 ml

Explain your thinking.

Undoing

Saya's swimming lesson lasts 50 minutes and it takes 15 minutes to change and get ready for the lesson. What time does Imran need to arrive if his lesson finishes at 6.15pm?

Explain thinking

The time is 10:35 am.
Jack says that the time is closer to 11:00am than to 10:00am.

Is Jack right?
Explain why.

Write more statements

One battery weighs the same as 60 paperclips;
One pencil sharpener weighs the same as 20 paperclips.
How many pencil sharpeners weigh the same as a battery?

Testing conditions

If the width of a rectangle is 3 metres less than the length, and the perimeter is between 20 and 30 metres, what could the dimensions of the rectangle be?

Convince me.

Buying tickets

Adult tickets cost £8 and children's tickets cost £4.
How many adult and children's tickets could I buy for £100 exactly?

Find more than one way of doing this.

Always, sometimes, never

If you double the area of a rectangle, you double the perimeter.

Working backwards

Put these times of the day in order, starting with the earliest time.

A: Quarter to four in the afternoon

B: 07:56

C: six minutes to nine in the evening

D: 14:36

The answer is...

The answer is ... 225 metres

What is the question?

What do you notice?

What do you notice?

1:00pm = 13:00
2:00pm = 14:00

Continue the pattern

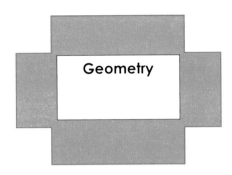

Geometry

Year 4: Geometry

Geometry	Compare and classify geometric shapes, including quadrilaterals and triangles, based on their properties and sizes.
	Identify acute and obtuse angles and compare and order angles up to two right angles by size.
	Identify lines of symmetry in 2-D shapes presented in different orientations.
	Complete a simple symmetric figure with respect to a specific line of symmetry.
	Describe positions on a 2-D grid as coordinates in the first quadrant. Describe movements between positions as translations of a given unit to the left/right and up/down.
	Plot specified points and draw sides to complete a given polygon.

Creating Patterns

Create an interesting pattern that includes at least 2 horizontal, 2 vertical and another set of parallel lines.

Design a Badge

Design a special badge by using at least 2 horizontal, 2 vertical and another set of parallel lines.

Design a sports badge by using at least 2 horizontal, 2 vertical and another set of parallel lines.

Visualising

Imagine a square cut along the diagonal to make two triangles.
Describe the triangles.
Join the triangles on different sides to make new shapes.
Describe them. (You could sketch them.)
Are any of the shapes symmetrical?
Convince me.

Symmetry

Draw a non-right angled triangle with a line of symmetry.

Always, sometimes, never

Is it always, sometimes or never true that the two diagonals of a rectangle meet at right angles?

Criteria of polygons

Show or draw a polygon that fits both of these criteria.

"Has exactly two equal sides."
"Has exactly two parallel sides."

What do you look for?

Working backwards

Here are the co-ordinates of corners of a rectangle which has width of 5.

(7, 3) and (27, 3)

What are the other two co-ordinates?

Convince me

John says that he can draw a right angled triangle which has another angle which is obtuse.

Is he right?

Explain why.

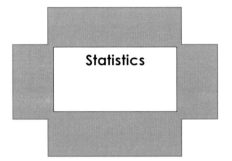

Statistics

Year 4: Statistics

Stats	Interpret and present discrete and continuous data using appropriate graphical methods, including bar charts and time graphs.
	Solve comparison, sum and difference problems using information presented in bar charts, pictograms, tables and other graphs.

Cleaning teeth

A group of children has created this table to show how long they spend brushing their teeth each day over a three-day period.

Pupil Name	Number of minutes brushing teeth each day		
	Day 1	Day 2	Day 3
Mary	5	2	8
Aysha	1	-	2
Nick	4	2	8
Tessa	3	2	3

Which child spends most time brushing his/her teeth over the three days?

Give a good reason why Aysha didn't record any time on Day 2.

Put, in order, which child spends the longest to the shortest amount of time brushing his/her teeth.

1_____   2_____   3_____   4_____

Teachers' cars

There are 6 teachers' cars on the school car park. The table below shows how many miles each car has travelled, how old it is and how much it is worth.

Car	Mileage	How old (years)	Value
Mr Ace	13, 000	2	£10,500
Mrs Bean	23, 500	6	£7,000
Ms Cold	24, 500	8	£4,500
Miss Eve	5,500	3	£17,500
Mr Frank	1,500	1	£22,000
Ms Gas	25,000	9	£1,500

Create the following graphs using any form you like.
a)   Create a graph to show the mileage covered by the cars.
b)   Create another graph to show the cars' values
c)   Create a third graph to show the age of the cars.

Keeping healthy and exercise

A group of children have created this table to show how they keep healthy by exercising. They show their best score in three different events.

Pupil Name	Number completed in a minute		
	Star Jumps	Sit ups	Press ups
Mary	16	8	10
Aysha	18	10	12
Nick	29	20	28
Tessa	13	2	3

Which child is best at all three?

Which exercise seems to be the most difficult?

Order the children according to their total score.

1_____ 2_____ 3_____ 4_____

World's tallest buildings

Class 3 did an investigation about tall buildings in different cities across the world. They started by looking at the tallest building in the UK and then compared it with 6 of the world's tallest buildings. Here is their chart:

Building Name	Height (m)	Number of floors
The Shard, London	306	72
Burj Khalifa	828	163
Shanghai Tower	632	121
Makka Tower Hotel	601	120
One World Trade Centre	541	104
CTF Finance Centre	530	111
Taipei 101	509	101

Create the following graphs using any form you like.

a) Create a graph to show the number of floors in each hotel.

b) Create another graph to show the height of each hotel.

c) How much taller is the Makka Tower Hotel than the Shard in London?

d) How many extra floors does the Shanghai Tower have compared with the Shard?

Roman soldiers

Roman soldiers moved between different forts. As can be seen from the table below each fort had soldiers that were there all year. Extra soldiers were brought in for the summer or winter months.

Roman Fort	Number of soldiers in each fort		
	All Year	October to March only	April to September only
Ambleside	3500	800	1000
Chester	18000	100	1200
Castleshaw	2900	200	280
Wreay	1300	200	350

Which fort held the most soldiers?

How many soldiers were there in Wreay fort in January?

Calculate how many soldiers were in each fort in July and put them in order (largest first).

1 _____ 2 _____ 3 _____ 4 _____

World's longest rivers

Class 7 did an investigation about the world's longest rivers. Here is a chart of their findings:

River	Length(m)	Continent
Nile	4,180	Africa
Amazon	3,912	South America
Mississippi - Missouri	3,710	North America
Chang Jeng (Yangtse)	3,602	Asia
Ob	3,459	Europe
Huang Ho	2,900	Asia
Yenisei	2,800	Europe
Parana	2,795	South America
Irtish	2,758	Europe
Zaire	2,716	Africa

*For the sake of this table Russia has been included in Europe.

How much longer is the Nile than the Yenisei?

Which is the longest river in Asia?

Using squared paper create a graph showing the 10 rivers by length and colour code them according to their continent.